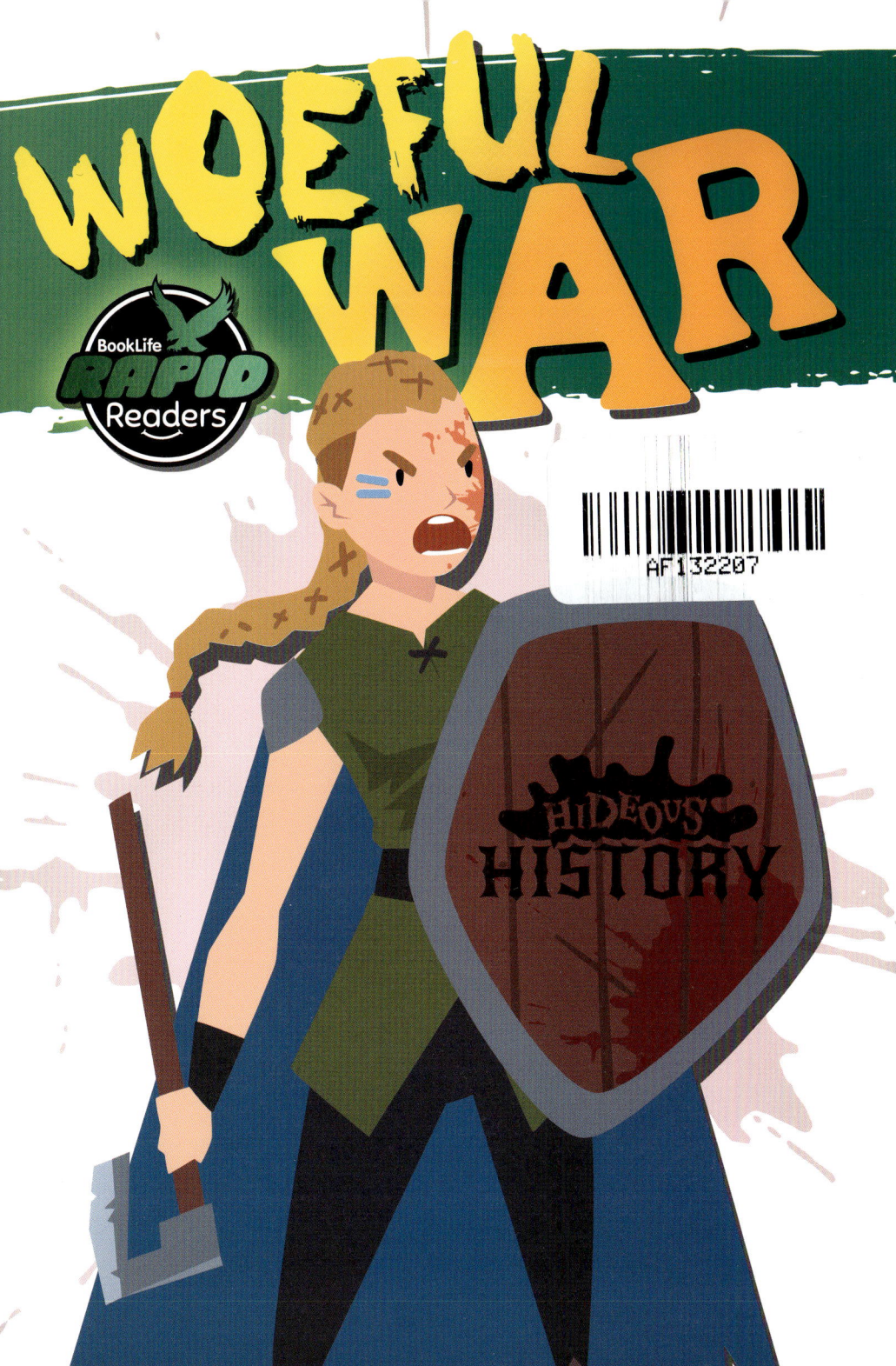

CONTENTS

PAGE 4   PIECES OF THE PAST

PAGE 6   BATTLE OF TOURS

PAGE 8   THE BATTLE OF HASTINGS

PAGE 10   NIGHT ATTACK AT TÂRGOVIȘTE

PAGE 12   THE SIEGE OF ORLEANS

PAGE 14   THE PUNIC WARS

PAGE 16   BATTLE OF BRITAIN

PAGE 18   THE NAPOLEONIC WARS

PAGE 20   WORLD WAR ONE

PAGE 22   THE BATTLE OF CAJAMARCA

PAGE 24	THE FRENCH REVOLUTION
PAGE 26	THE GREAT EMU WAR
PAGE 28	THE BATTLE OF THERMOPYLAE
PAGE 30	HIDEOUS HISTORY
PAGE 31	GLOSSARY
PAGE 32	INDEX

Words that look like this are explained in the glossary on page 31.

Photo Credits
Images are courtesy of Shutterstock.com. With thanks to Getty Images, Thinkstock Photo and iStockphoto.
Front Cover – NotionPic, Stasia04, Everett Collection, Ekaterina Bykova. 4–5 – kamomeen, zef art, VikiVector. 6–7 – Hervé Champollion / akg-images. 8–9 – jorisvo, Vectors Bang. 10–11 – Gabi80, delcarmat, Nicoleta Ionescu, Fotokon. 12–13 – Nancy Bauer, Everett Collection, Steven Hodel, S_O_Va. 14–15 – Sammy33, Massimo Todaro, Vuk Kostic. 16–17 – Steve Walker Photography, oculo. 20–21 – rahalarts. 22–23 – Thomas Wyness, Luis Alberto Pena ramos. 24–25 – SexyMandalaMan, Adwo. 26–27 – TownFox, Jackie Babe, Anan Kaewkhammul. 28–29 – A.Davey, CC BY 2.0, via Wikimedia Commons, yiannisscheidt. 30 – zef art.

BookLife PUBLISHING

©2023
BookLife Publishing Ltd.
King's Lynn, Norfolk
PE30 4LS, UK

All rights reserved.
Printed in Poland.

A catalogue record for this book is available from the British Library.

ISBN: 978-1-80155-891-4

Written by:
Hermione Redshaw

Edited by:
William Anthony

Designed by:
Drue Rintoul

All facts, statistics, web addresses and URLs in this book were verified as valid and accurate at time of writing.
No responsibility for any changes to external websites or references can be accepted by either the author or publisher.

PIECES OF THE PAST

There are secrets underground. It's not all dirt and mud if you know where to look. Buried under all that earth are clues to the past.

The past was not a nice place to live. There were plenty of things people needed to avoid to reach old age.

Towns were dirty. Work was brutal. Disease and war were everywhere. Yet, people still lived their lives.

Let's take a journey into the past. Are you ready to learn about the hideous history of woeful war? You will have to be brave...

BATTLE OF TOURS

In AD 732, there was a large army from Spain. It was made up of people called Moors. They rode their horses through Gaul, an area of Europe at the time.

Their leader, Abdul al-Rahman, wanted them to take over more of Europe. So far, it had been pretty easy. That was all about to change.

The Frank army wanted to protect Gaul. However, they were much smaller and didn't have any horses. The two armies met near the towns of Tours.

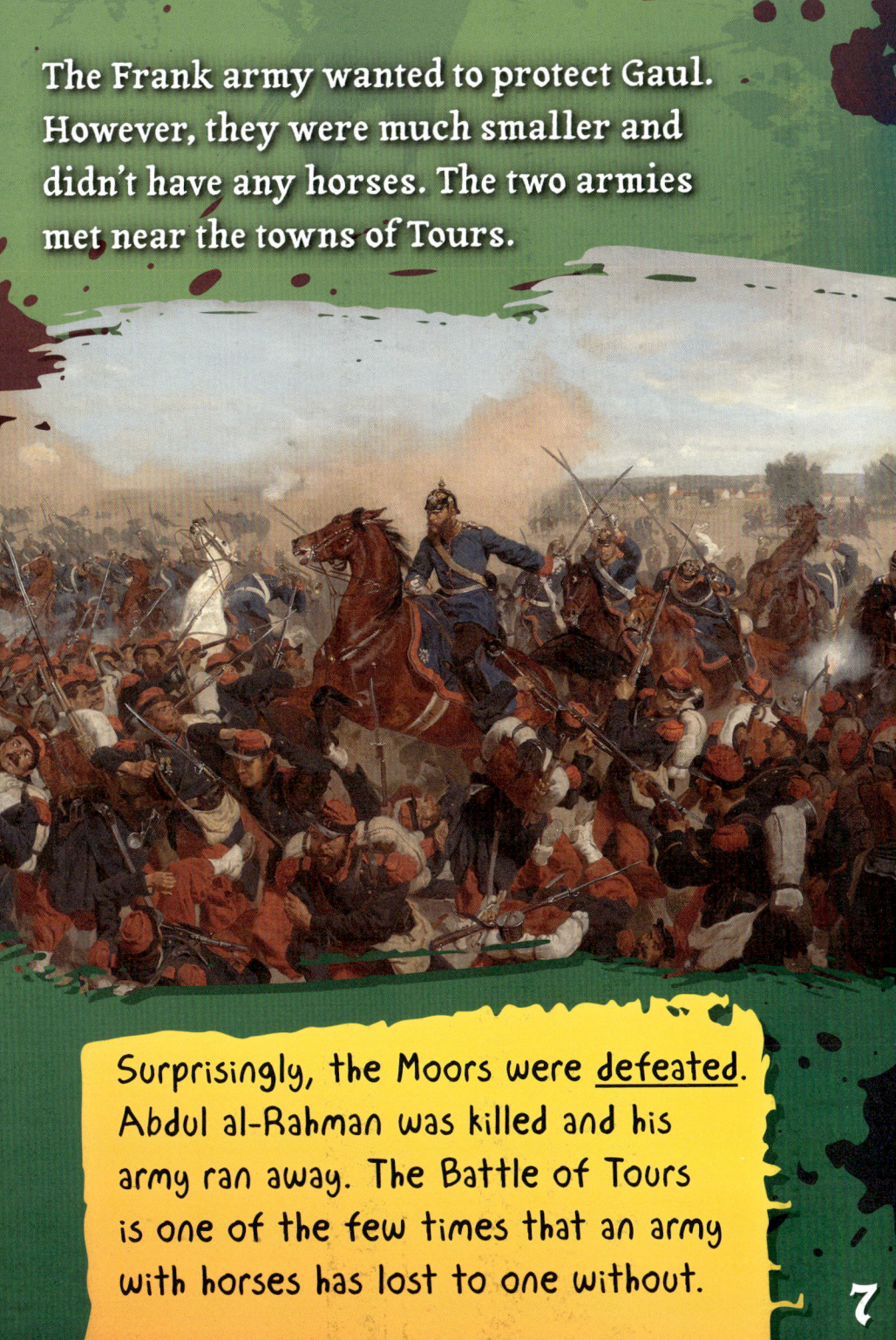

Surprisingly, the Moors were <u>defeated</u>. Abdul al-Rahman was killed and his army ran away. The Battle of Tours is one of the few times that an army with horses has lost to one without.

THE BATTLE OF HASTINGS

After King Edward the Confessor died, Harold Godwinson was crowned King Harold II of England. However, some others also wanted to be king.

Harald Hardrada came to England with 300 Viking ships. They attacked from the north and <u>conquered</u> the city of York. Harold Godwinson marched his army all the way there from the south. He killed Hardrada and his men.

Harold and his army travelled back south quickly to fight William of Normandy. Harold's soldiers were tired by the time they reached Hastings.

William of Normandy had a large army and 700 ships. William's <u>cavalry</u> killed most of Harold's army. It is said that Harold was shot in the eye with an arrow. William was crowned king on Christmas Day, 1066.

A NIGHT ATTACK AT TÂRGOVIȘTE

Vlad the Impaler ruled Wallachia, an old country in what is now Eastern Europe. He did many terrible things. However, nothing compared to what he did in 1462.

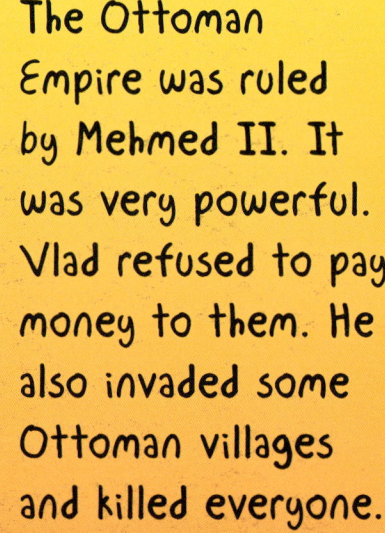

The Ottoman Empire was ruled by Mehmed II. It was very powerful. Vlad refused to pay money to them. He also invaded some Ottoman villages and killed everyone.

Mehmed's army invaded Wallachia. They set up tents when they got near the capital. Vlad decided to kill Mehmed in the night, but attacked the wrong tent! He was chased away.

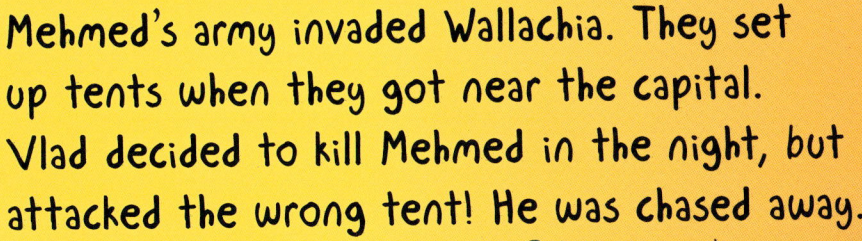

The next day, the Ottomans found no soldiers. Instead, they found a forest of around 20,000 dead Ottoman prisoners. They had all been <u>impaled</u> on stakes.

Now you know how Vlad the Impaler got his name.

THE SIEGE OF ORLEANS

Joan lived on a farm in France. In 1425, when Joan was 13, she started hearing voices from heaven. The voices told her that she needed to help the French king and save France.

At the time, England and France were fighting each other in what was known as the Hundred Years' War. It had started in 1337 and England looked to be winning.

In 1428, the voices told Joan to meet the French king, Charles VII. Charles believed that she had been sent by God to help him win the war.

Joan of Arc, as she was now known, was sent to Orleans. She and her army chased the English away from several fortresses around Orleans. The French soldiers were <u>inspired</u> by Joan.

THE PUNIC WARS

The Punic Wars were between the Romans and the Carthaginians. The Carthaginians came from North Africa, but controlled parts of Spain.

Hannibal became the new leader of the Carthaginians' Spanish army. When he was a boy, he had sworn to destroy Rome. In 216 BC, he marched an army across Europe to attack it.

The Alps is a huge mountain range in Europe. Nobody expected Hannibal to travel through it to get to Italy. The Romans were caught by surprise.

The Roman army was nearly twice as big as Hannibal's. However, Hannibal was a clever general. He managed to surround the Romans with his horses. They were trapped! The Carthaginians <u>slaughtered</u> the Romans.

BATTLE OF BRITAIN

In 1940, Winston Churchill said:

> Never, in the field of human conflict, was so much owed to so many by so few.

Churchill was talking about the Battle of Britain.

The British air force and the German air force fought in the skies over Britain. Everyone was grateful to the few pilots who defended their country from the skies.

The Battle of Britain lasted 112 days, according to records. It was the first all-air battle in history. The British were outnumbered. However, they fought off Germany and protected the people of Britain.

The British were stronger than the Germans thought. Nowadays, the pilots who fought in the Battle of Britain are known as 'The Few' because of Churchill's speech.

THE NAPOLEONIC WARS

One of the greatest war generals in history was a man named Napoleon Bonaparte. He was famous for his clever strategies and important victories. In 1799, he ended the French Revolution and became leader of France.

The Napoleonic Wars happened from 1803 to 1815. Napoleon tried to make things stable again during a messy time in French history.

In 1805, Napoleon defeated the Austrians and Russians. The leaders of some other countries were loyal to him. This meant that Napoleon had control over many areas of Europe.

Then, Napoleon had some costly defeats and failures. The capital of France was taken over in 1814. Napoleon was finally defeated by the British near the village of Waterloo in 1815.

WORLD WAR ONE

World War One was fought between 1914 and 1918. One side included Germany, Austria-Hungary, Bulgaria and the Ottoman Empire. The other side included France, Britain, Russia, Italy and Japan.

Lots of new <u>technology</u> was invented and perfected to fight the war, such as tanks, chemical weapons and new machine guns. World War One was also famous for its trenches.

Trenches were long, narrow ditches dug into the ground. Each side had their own trenches on the battlefield.

The land in between the trenches was called No Man's Land.

There was more to worry about in the trenches than enemy soldiers. Toilets overflowed, dead bodies lay nearby and there were rats everywhere. Many soldiers got an <u>infection</u> called trench foot.

THE BATTLE OF CAJAMARCA

In 1532, Atahualpa became leader of the Incas. He had just won a war against his half-brother and was waiting for him to be brought to the town of Cajamarca.

Meanwhile, a small group of Spanish soldiers were travelling nearby. They were led by a man called Pizarro. They had guns and horses, which many of the Inca people had never seen.

Pizarro and his men formed a plan to capture Atahualpa. Pizarro hid his cannons and horses behind buildings as he met Atahualpa at the town square.

The Spanish handed Atahualpa a prayer book and told them him God. He threw it away in disgust. So, Pizarro's soldiers opened fire.

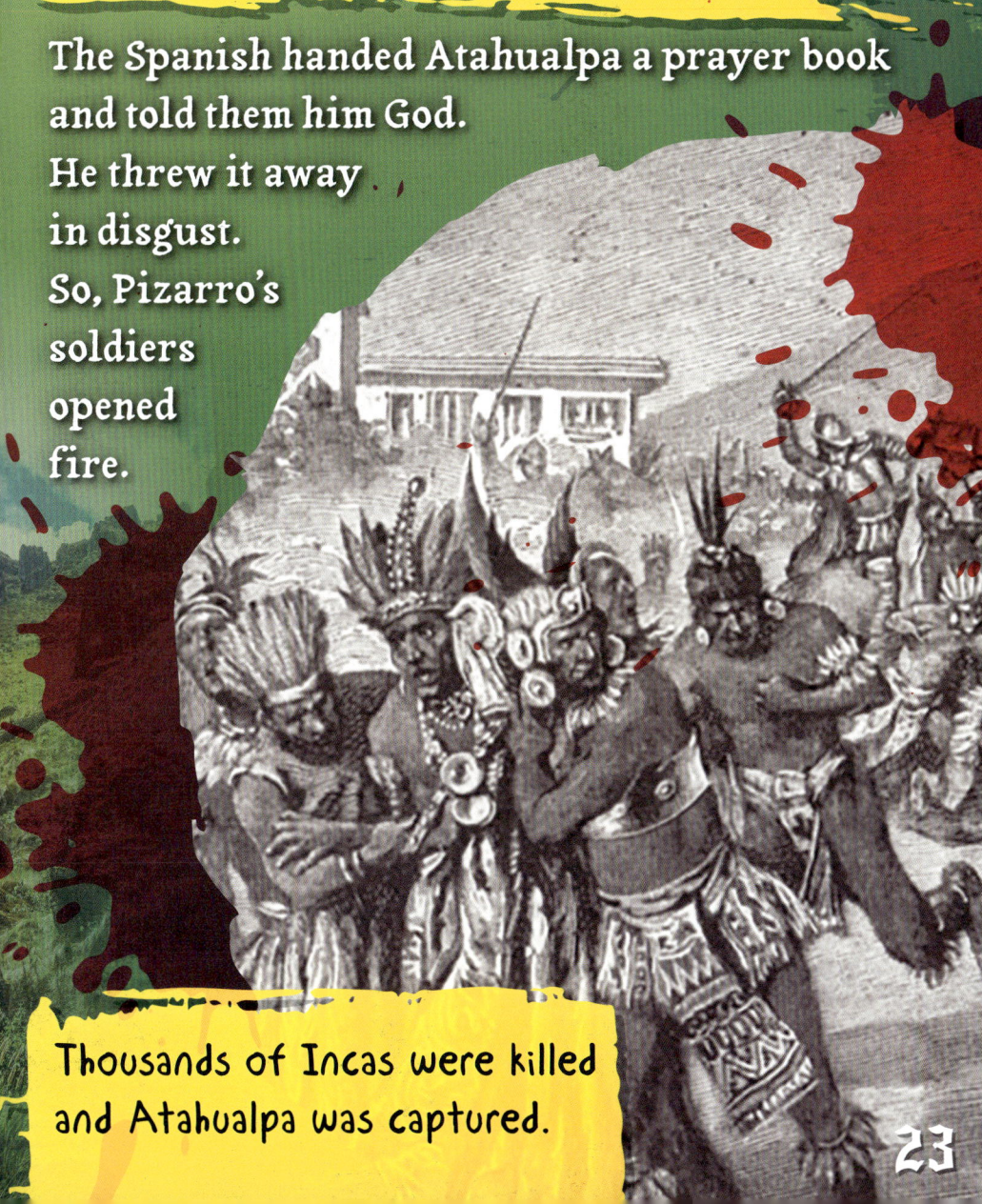

Thousands of Incas were killed and Atahualpa was captured.

THE FRENCH REVOLUTION

Not all wars are between different countries. Sometimes, a country can have a war with itself. This can be called a civil war or a revolution.

One of the nastiest revolutions was the French Revolution. There were three different groups of people in France, called estates. They were the clergy, the nobles and the peasants.

The Revolution started when peasants stormed a fortress called the Bastille to steal gunpowder and weapons. They burned down the houses of tax collectors and rich people. Eventually, they took over the country.

In 1793, the king was arrested for <u>treason</u> and <u>beheaded</u>. The last queen of France, Marie Antoinette, was killed the same way. The Revolution changed France forever.

THE GREAT EMU WAR

After World War One, thousands of Australian soldiers had returned home to find that they couldn't get another job. The government offered these soldiers homes and farms all over the country.

However, farming in Australia was difficult at the time. The biggest problem wasn't drought or money. It was emus.

Emus are giant, flightless birds. There were about 20,000 in Australia.

Emus roamed the country, eating wheat and tearing down fences. The farmers tried to deal with the emus themselves but had to give up. The emus were too strong.

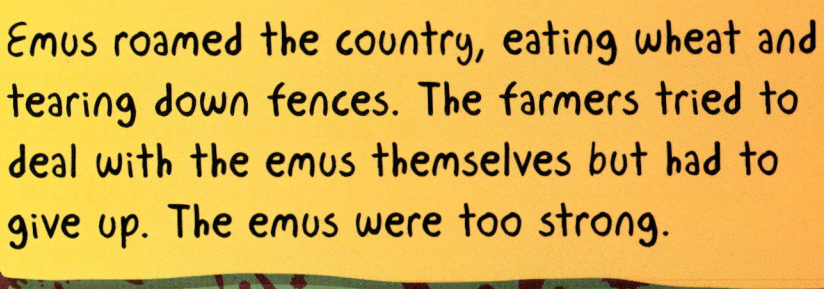

It was time to declare war on the emus. The Australians sent a small group of soldiers to kill the birds. However, the battle went badly. The emus won.

THE BATTLE OF THERMOPYLAE

In 480 BC, Persia had a huge empire with massive armies. The king of Persia, Xerxes, invaded Greece because he wanted more land. However, the Greeks would not give up their country.

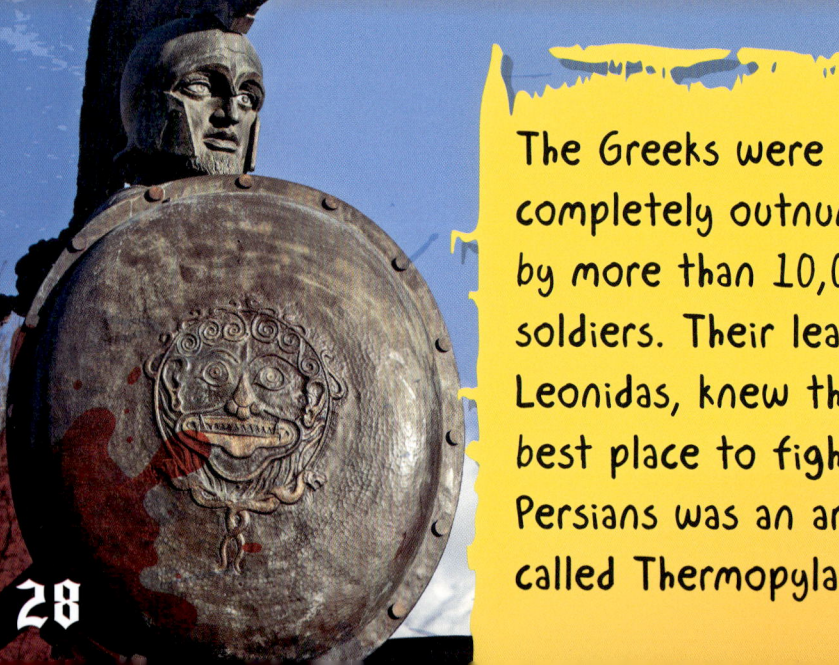

The Greeks were completely outnumbered by more than 10,000 soldiers. Their leader, Leonidas, knew that the best place to fight the Persians was an area called Thermopylae.

Thermopylae was perfect because it was a stretch of narrow land next to the sea. This meant that the Persian forces couldn't surround the Greeks. Their bigger army would be useless.

The Greeks defended their position well and few were killed. However, then a man called Ephialtes betrayed them. He told Xerxes of a secret path that led around Thermopylae.

HIDEOUS HISTORY

Take a deep breath. Allow yourself to calm down. The past was a dreadful place, but it is not where you live now.

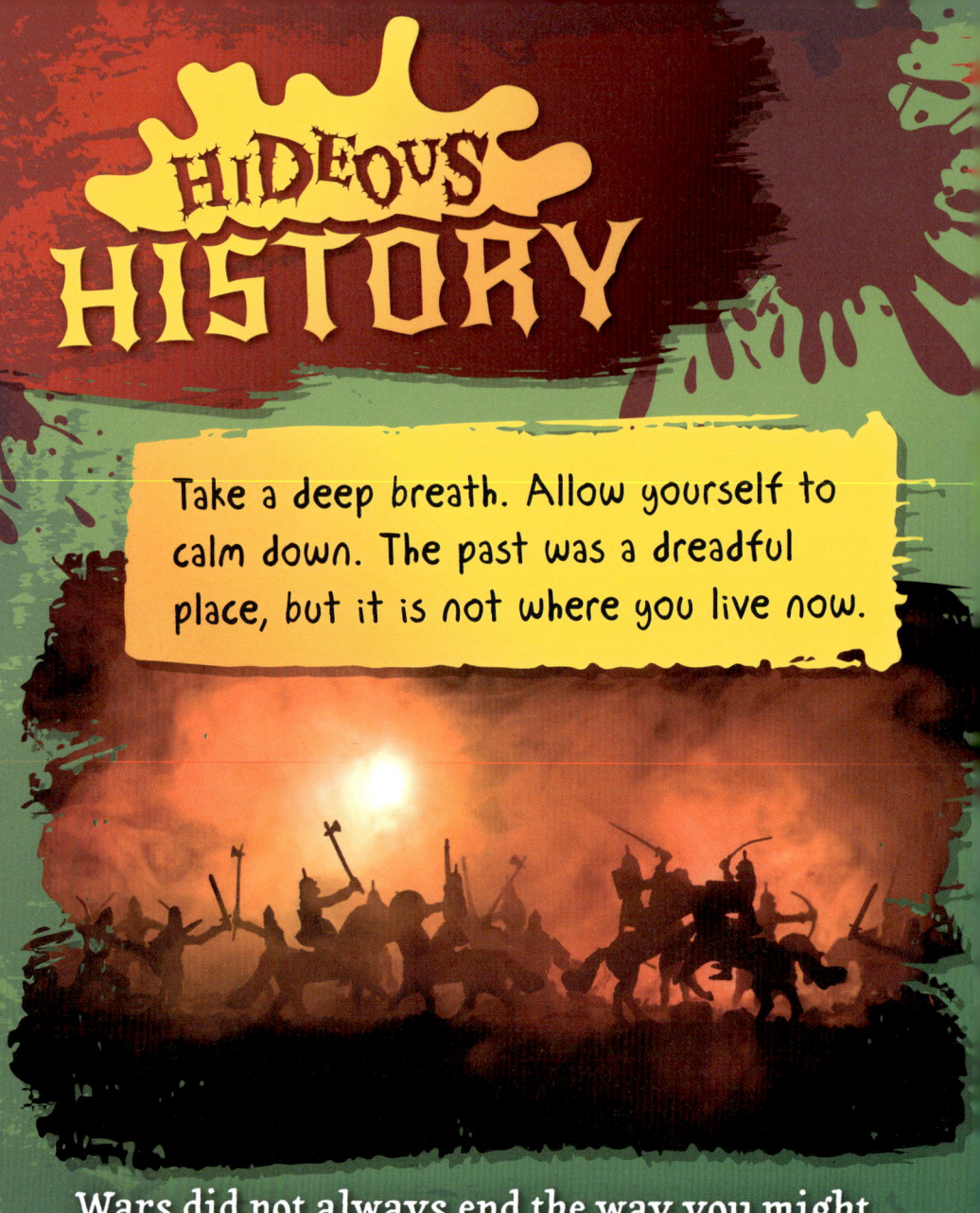

Wars did not always end the way you might have expected. Many people met a brutal end. These stories showed that whether you were a king or a peasant, no one is safe from war.

GLOSSARY

BEHEADED had their head cut off

CAVALRY the parts of an army that serve on horseback

CONQUERED Taken control of somewhere through the use of force

DEFEATED failed or lost

IMPALED had a pointed object forced through a part of the body

INFECTION an illness caused by germs getting into the body

INSPIRED created a feeling in other people in which they believed they could do something great

SLAUGHTERED killed in a violent way

TECHNOLOGY machines or devices that are made using scientific knowledge

TREASON a crime where someone betrays their country

INDEX

ARMIES 6–9, 11, 13–15, 28–29

FARMING 26

HORSES 6–7, 15, 22–23

KINGS 8–9, 12–13, 25, 28, 30

PILOTS 16–17

QUEENS 25

REVOLUTIONS 18, 24–25

SOLDIERS 9, 11, 13, 21–23, 26–28

TRENCHES 20–21

WEAPONS 20, 25

AN INTRODUCTION TO BOOKLIFE RAPID READERS...

Packed full of gripping topics and twisted tales, BookLife Rapid Readers are perfect for older children looking to propel their reading up to top speed. With three levels based on our planet's fastest animals, children will be able to find the perfect point from which to accelerate their reading journey. From the spooky to the silly, these roaring reads will turn every child at every reading level into a prolific page-turner!

CHEETAH
The fastest animals on land, cheetahs will be taking their first strides as they race to top speed.

MARLIN
The fastest animals under water, marlins will be blasting through their journey.

FALCON
The fastest animals in the air, falcons will be flying at top speed as they tear through the skies.